Mapping the World

VOLUME 8

MAPPING FOR TODAY AND TOMORROW

GROLIER
EDUCATIONAL

Published 2002 by Grolier Educational, Danbury, CT 06816

This edition published exclusively for the school and library market

Produced by Andromeda Oxford Limited
11–13 The Vineyard, Abingdon,
Oxon OX14 3PX, U.K.

Copyright © Andromeda Oxford Limited 2002

Contributors: *Peter Evea, Stella Douglas, Peter Elliot, David Fairbairn, Ian Falconer*

Project Consultant: *Dr. David Fairbairn, Lecturer in Geomatics, University of Newcastle-upon-Tyne, England*

Project Director: *Graham Bateman*
Managing Editor: *Shaun Barrington*
Design Manager: *Frankie Wood*
Editorial Assistant: *Marian Dreier*
Picture Researcher: *David Pratt*
Picture Manager: *Claire Turner*
Production: *Clive Sparling*
Index: *Janet Dudley*

Design and origination by Gecko

Printed in Hong Kong

Set ISBN 0-7172-5619-7

Library of Congress Cataloging-in-Publication Data

Mapping the world.
   p. cm.
Includes index.
Contents: v. 1. Ways of mapping the world --v. 2. Observation and measurement -- v. 3. Maps for travelers -- v. 4. Navigation -- v. 5. Mapping new lands -- v. 6. Mapping for governments -- v. 7. City maps -- v. 8. Mapping for today and tomorrow.
ISBN 0-7172-5619-7 (set : alk. paper)
   1. Cartography--Juvenile literature. [1. Cartogaphy. Maps.] I. Grolier Educational (Firm)

GA105.6 .M37 2002
562--dc21

2001051229

Contents

About This Set

Mapping the World is an eight-volume set that describes the history of cartography, discusses its importance in the development of different cultures, and explains how it is done. Cartography is the technique of compiling information for, and then drawing, maps or charts. Each volume examines a particular aspect of mapping and is illustrated by numerous artworks and photographs selected to help understanding of the sometimes complex themes.

After all, cartography is both a science and an art. It has existed since before words were written down and today uses the most up-to-date computer technology and imaging systems. It is vital to governments in peacetime and in wartime, as much as to the individual business person, geologist, vacationer–or pirate! Advances in mapmaking through history have been closely involved with wider advances in science and technology. It demands some understanding of math and at the same time an appreciation of visual creativity. Such a subject is bound to get a little complex at times!

What Is a Map?

We all think we know, but the word is surprisingly difficult to define. "A representation of the earth, or part of the earth, or another part of the universe–usually on a flat surface–that shows a group of features in terms of their relative size and position." But even this long-winded attempt is not the whole story: As explained in Volume 1, most early cultures tried to map the unseen–the underworld, the realms of gods, or the unknown structure of the cosmos. Maps are not just ink on paper or lines on a computer screen. They can be "mental maps." And the problem of mapping a round object–the earth or one of the planets–on a flat surface means that there is no perfect flat map, one that shows precise "size and position."

The cartographer has to compromise to show relative location, direction, and area in the best way

for a specific purpose. He or she must decide what information to include and what to leave out: A sea chart is very different from a subway map. This set explains how the information is gathered–by surveying, for example–and how the cartographer makes decisions about scale, map projection, symbols, and all other aspects of mapmaking.

Researching a Subject

Separate topics in the set are presented in sections of from two to six pages so that your understanding of the subject grows in a logical way. Words and phrases in *italic* are explained more fully in the glossaries. Each glossary is specific to one volume. There is a set index in each volume. Recommended further reading and websites are also listed in each volume. At the bottom of each left-hand page there are cross-references to other sections in the set that expand on some aspect of the subject under discussion.

By consulting the index and cross-references, you can follow a particular topic across the set volumes. Each volume takes a different approach. For example, different aspects of the work of the famous mapmaker Gerardus Mercator are discussed in several volumes: the mathematical basis of his map projection in Volume 2, his importance for navigation in Volume 4, and his success as a businessman in Volume 5.

The continuous effort to improve mapping is part of the history of exploration, navigation, warfare, politics, and technology. All of these subjects–and many more–are discussed in *Mapping the World*.

Maps and artworks help explain technical points in the text

Cross-references to other relevant sections in the set give section title, volume number, and page references

Introduction to Volume 8

Today, mapmaking is computerized, and map coordinates can be combined with other data to create a geographical information system (GIS). GIS can include pictures, such as air photographs and satellite images. Our information about the physical world is now highly accurate, and we can make maps of different landscapes with many different themes. Our maps of the solar system are continually improving as space probes provide more and better information. Maps no longer have to be printed on paper: The Internet means that maps can be distributed anywhere in the world cheaply and efficiently.

Aspects of the section subject are sometimes explained in separate information boxes

Photographs and illustrations of people, locations, instruments–and, of course, maps–add to the text information

Summary introduces the section topic

Main entry heading to a two-, four-, or six-page section

Each volume is color-coded

Calculating Longitude

For a long time sailors were able to work out their latitude, or position relative to the equator. While explorers kept in sight of the coast, there was little need to calculate how far they had traveled in an easterly or westerly direction. However, as explorers traveled further away from home, they needed more and more to know their longitude.

Lines of longitude, called *meridians*, are imaginary lines on the earth's surface running directly from the North Pole to the South Pole. Longitude is measured eastward and westward from the Prime Meridian (0°). In 1884 an international agreement fixed this line to run through Greenwich in London, England. The longitude of a point is the angle at the center of the earth between the meridian on which it lies and the Prime Meridian. The degrees are numbered west and east of Greenwich up to 180°. Establishing position in an east-west direction was

historically much more difficult than working out a ship's latitude, and for centuries sailors could do no more than estimate their longitude, often not very accurately, using dead reckoning (see page 11).

Early methods of trying to measure longitude involved noting the distances of certain stars from the moon or observing the orbits of Jupiter's moons, but none was accurate enough. It is possible to calculate longitude by using the position of the stars. However, the problem with this method is that the stars shift their position eastward every day. To use their positions to calculate your own position, you need to know the precise local time relative to a fixed reference point.

The earth turns 360° (a complete revolution) every day and 15° every hour. If a navigator knew the time in Greenwich, England, which is on the Prime Meridian, or 0° of longitude, and also knew the precise local time, it would be simple math to multiply the time difference (in hours) by 15 to give

John Harrison 1693–1776

In 1714 the British Board of Longitude announced a competition. Whoever could invent a method for accurately finding a ship's longitude would win a huge prize of £20,000. The government was not giving away such a large amount of money for nothing. Being able to calculate longitude could provide enormous advantages in international trading and military seapower, to say nothing of helping prevent disasters at sea resulting from poor navigation. To win the prize, the ship's longitude had to be measured to an accuracy of 0.5 degrees, or 30 minutes, of longitude. Harrison knew that he could win if he could produce a very accurate marine clock, or chronometer. His fourth, brilliant design proved to be accurate enough to win the competition. It was tested at sea during 1761 and 1762, and experiments found that over a 5-month period it had an error of just 1.25 minutes of longitude, easily accurate enough to win the prize.

▲▲ Harrison with an earlier clock (above) and the compact design of his fourth model (left).

the ship's longitude. To do this, there had to be an accurate way of measuring time.

Johan Werner first suggested using some sort of timekeeper as early as 1514 but was not able to build one that had enough accuracy. Until John Harrison's designs clocks had to be constantly adjusted. And the problem was even worse at sea, with changes in temperature, dampness, and the ship's movement all upsetting a clock's delicate mechanism. Harrison succeeded in overcoming all these problems. His development of the marine chronometer in the 18th century finally allowed navigators to accurately determine their longitude. By referring to nautical almanacs that were compiled by astronomical observatories, the navigators could work out their position east or west as well as north or south.

◄ World time zones. The time changes by one hour for every 15° of longitude traveled around the earth. You lose or gain a day crossing the International Date Line.

Time Zones

Because the earth spins by 15° of longitude every hour, anyone traveling in a westerly direction will lengthen the day by one hour for every 15° of longitude traveled. Similarly, traveling eastward will shorten the day by one hour. This distance is a long way at the equator, but less and less the further south or north you are. A sailor could not continue to gain or lose time for ever, so in 1884 a Canadian engineer called Sir Sandford Fleming suggested a system of time zones (see diagram on page 20). He also proposed the International Date Line. This line runs north-south through the Pacific Ocean and avoids major landmasses. When a traveler crosses the line going westward (say, flying from Los Angeles to Sydney), a day is added. Nine on the morning of June 10 immediately becomes 9 a.m. on June 11. In the opposite direction (for example, from Auckland in New Zealand to Honolulu) 9 a.m. on June 11 becomes 9 a.m. on June 10.

21

See Also: Latitude, Longitude, and Positioning 2: 26–29; Finding Your Way on the Ocean 4: 10–11

20

Captions explain context of illustrations

Digital Mapping

There has been a revolution in mapping in the last 30 years. Until the 1970s almost every map was created by hand. A cartographer either took the measurements from surveys and converted them into a map, drawing the symbols herself and deciding on the overall design; or the cartographer would redraw using other maps as a starting point. Today, almost all maps are computer-generated, which has several advantages over the old method.

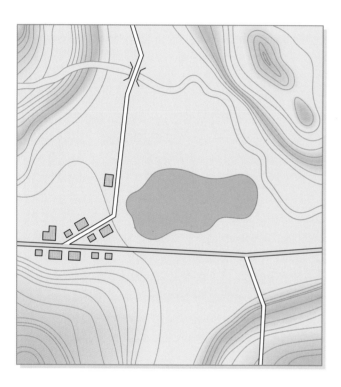

▲ This map was drawn by hand using pen and ink. For hand-drawn maps to be to be printed, the draftsman had to prepare a different sheet for each color on the map–in this case the black, yellow, and blue detail. (The green features were drawn on both the blue and yellow sheet and showed green in those overlapping areas in the printed version.)

▶ The same data can be displayed in a computer software package. Here the detail has been drawn simply. The information held in the computer is a list of coordinates (positions) of each point or bend in a line or outline of an area. The coordinates are plotted and joined together to create this basic map.

Before the use of computers cartographers had to be highly skilled draftsmen and draftswomen. They had many years of training in producing symbols and lettering on maps. Twentieth-century developments in the printing industry helped speed up the reproduction of maps. It was possible to produce many thousands of copies, for example, in school atlases or for gas companies to give out to traveling motorists. The original drawing, however, was the work of one skilled cartographer or a team of cartographers that was able to produce a high-quality map suitable to be printed in many copies.

New Kinds of "Customized" Maps

Today people want maps that are suitable only for themselves, and for the first time that is possible. If you want a special map showing how to travel from your home to the football stadium, it is unlikely to be printed in thousands of copies because only you are interested in it. If someone else wanted a map of the same area and even the same journey as you do, they may want different features shown on it. They may travel from your neighborhood to the stadium by car, following road names and numbers. You, on

SEE ALSO: *MAP MATERIALS THROUGH HISTORY* **1**: *18–19*; *USING COORDINATES* **2**: *30–31*

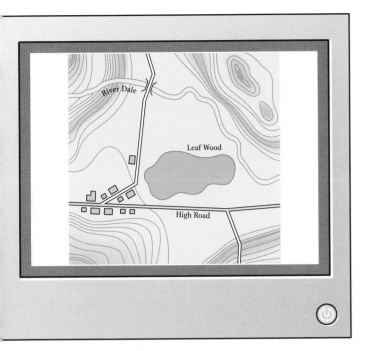

◀ The computer software can help design as well as plot detail. Here the map has been made to look exactly the same as the hand-drawn map on page 6. Text has been added and the design can be easily altered.

▼ As well as holding the map coordinates, the computer can also retain an enormous amount of information in its database about the *attributes,* or properties, of the features shown, like names, to be called up as needed.

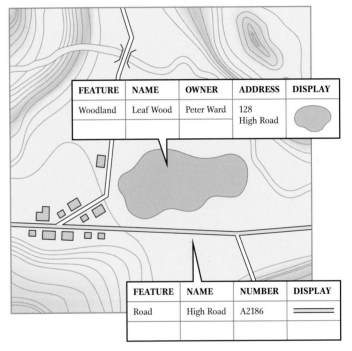

FEATURE	NAME	OWNER	ADDRESS	DISPLAY
Woodland	Leaf Wood	Peter Ward	128 High Road	

FEATURE	NAME	NUMBER	DISPLAY
Road	High Road	A2186	

the other hand, may travel to the stadium using public transportation, so you may want the bus stops and routes shown on your map.

Some people use maps only to check that they are on the right route. Other people want to use a map alongside other information to test a theory or explore an idea. Someone traveling on a bus does not want the same kind of map as a scientist examining climate change.

Although many thousands of maps have been printed over hundreds of years, the cost of printing has limited the scope of the cartographer for "customizing" a map for only a very few people.

Printed maps in books are not only expensive and bulky, they date quite quickly. Some people prefer to look at a map on a TV screen, then "switch it off."

Maps today can be produced for smaller groups of people. The map can be changed to show different features. The same map can be made to look different by changing the design. Or maps can be combined with other information. And many maps can "disappear" when you press the "off" switch. It is not difficult to guess what new tool has made all this possible.

Computers and Maps

The development of new types of maps and map uses has happened because of computers. Today, instead of all maps being drawn by hand, almost all maps are produced using computer technology. Digital mapping is the name given to this computer-assisted cartography. It lets us create the kind of maps needed today, and it has further advantages.

Maps can be drawn more quickly using a computer than by hand. Also, it is usually cheaper to produce a map using a computer. You do not need the training in drawing that previous cartographers had: It is much easier for anyone to produce a good-quality map using a computer.

Computers were developed to help handle large amounts of data and make lots of calculations. They store and present information in the form of numbers. In order to use computers in mapping, we have to convert the information we have about the world into numbers. We also have to make sure that the computer is able to reproduce the symbols and design of a map on a screen.

Points, Lines, and Areas in the Computer

The task of converting our information about the real world into a form suitable for the computer is called *digitizing*. The numbers that are stored are the positions of features as they would appear on the map. These positions are called coordinates, and a digital map can consist of just a series of coordinates. The coordinates could be stored on their own, as a list of positions of points, for example. But they could also be stored as a series of successive points in order to define a line. If the last point of a series of points is the same as the first point, then the line joins back onto itself and defines an area.

So, the three main types of feature on a map—points, lines, and areas—can be stored in a computer as a set of coordinates. Once they are in the computer memory, called a database, we can run a computer program that will draw them onto the computer screen. Such a program is part of a *software* package that handles *computer graphics*.

Additional Design Information

If you were to plot out onto the screen, using the computer graphics program, a set of coordinates from the database, it is likely that you would see a black screen with some white areas, lines, and points on it. They would be accurately positioned representations of features on the earth's surface, but they would not look like a well-designed map. What is needed is some additional information beyond the simple coordinates to tell the computer how to design the look of the map.

The database with the coordinates can also store other information about the features. It can hold design information, such as "the line shown by these coordinates will be drawn in red" or "the color inside this area is light green." A very large amount of information like this can be stored, including the type of point symbol, the thickness of a line, or the shading pattern for an area.

The database can also include the name of a feature, so that the type of symbol that is usually added last to a map, the lettering, can be included on the computer-drawn map automatically.

Digitizing

It would take a long time to use a keyboard to type in all the coordinates of features in the real world. Databases are able to receive information supplied by a *GPS receiver*. A series of positions is recorded by the receiver as, for example, the GPS user walks along a road. That series of coordinates is fed directly into the computer, which uses them to add the road to the map in progress.

But the largest store of coordinate information actually comes from maps that have already been produced. Digital mapping relies on databases that have been created by transforming, or digitizing, paper maps.

Digitizing from paper maps is a very long and tedious operation; but once the information is in the database, it is very useful. A computer-based device called a *digitizing tablet* is normally used to convert the positions of features on a map into coordinates in a database. The map is laid on the digitizing tablet, and a pointing device, called a cursor, is used by the operator to position points, follow lines, or move around areas. Every time the operator presses a button at a point on the map, the coordinates are sent from the tablet to the database.

A set of feature coordinates with some extra information about the feature, such as its name or the color it should be plotted, is called *vector data*.

SEE ALSO: *THREE-DIMENSIONAL MAPPING* **1**: *30–33; ELECTRONIC CHARTS* **4**: *26–29*

Some Advantages of Digital Maps

In addition to holding the usual map information of point, line, and area (like the maps on pages 6 and 7), digital mapping can capture and manipulate other information.

Here the positions and heights of points on the landscape have been measured and digitized by surveyors "in the field." Back in the office the digital mapping software has created a pattern of triangles between the points surveyed. In the map on the right the software has traced *contours* through the array of points, transforming the map of the landscape relief into a line map.

Once this information is available, it can be passed on to the type of geographic information system explained on pages 10–11. The cartographer can now highlight areas above a certain height by a simple instruction to the computer. Different displays can be prepared. Each of the triangles defines an area of even slope and aspect (direction of slope), so "hill shading" can be automatically created. The map scale can be changed with a few keystrokes on the computer, as here: The right-hand map is smaller scale.

Imagine that this hilly area is a forest. The foresters want to log all the trees, but their logging machinery can only move across slopes that are not too steep. The computer can calculate which of the triangles of land can be crossed by the machinery and highlight them. With the right software it can even recommend the most efficient order in which to clear the trees.

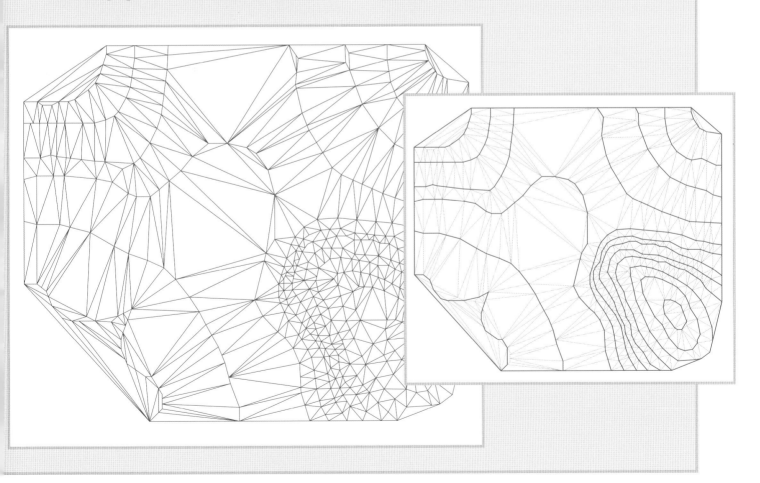

Geographic Information Systems

Computer databases can store lots of information that traditionally appears on maps. The coordinates in a database define the positions of features, and additional codes can tell the computer graphics software how to draw the features on the screen. Beyond the coordinates and their drawing codes there is almost no limit to the extra information that can be included in the database.

On a paper map you could identify a building and perhaps have enough space to write in the type of building (for example, shopping mall) and its name (Meadow Grove Shopping Center).

In a database, however, you could include much more information than you could ever add to a paper map. First, the shopping mall would have the coordinates of its shape and perhaps a code showing what color it should be drawn.

But the database could also hold the type of feature ("shopping mall") and its name ("Meadow Grove"). It might record the details of the owner ("John Smith Retail Properties Inc.") and a list of all the tenants in the mall ("Happy Feet Shoe Shop"; "Take-a-Break Coffee House"; "Apple@The Grove Computer Supplies"; "Mighty Bright Supermarket," etc.). In addition it could include the rent paid by each shop or the average counts of shoppers in different parts of the mall on different days.

The database could tell you how busy the parking lots are at different times of day, details of the nearest shops that provide competition, the layout of electrical and water services in the mall, and even the cleaning schedule used by the manager who keeps the mall tidy.

An enormous amount of information can be stored along with the map data in the computer. This combination of map detail and other related

► This is a map drawn from a very large database of information about the city of La Grande, Oregon. The database is the core of the city geographic information system, which can plot maps like this showing a lot of detail of the streets in the city center. This map was produced to show the impact of diesel pollution.

CITY OF LA GRANDE
Diesel Impact Area

Legend

☐ MAP: City Limits	—— MAP: Highways
☐ MAP: UGB	·····+··· MAP: RailRoad
☐ MAP: Diesel	—— MAP: Rivers

Properties on the periphery may be only partially impacted; however, entire blocks are highlighted.

Feet
0 200 400 600 800

1" = 350'
11/01/99 01.32 PM

SEE ALSO: *LAYERING INFORMATION* **2:** *10–11; APPLICATIONS OF GIS* **8:** *12–15*

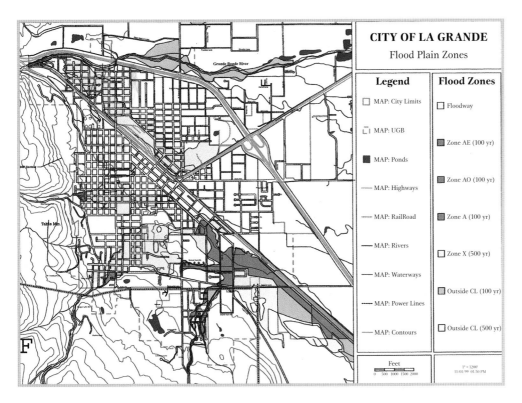

CITY OF LA GRANDE
Flood Plain Zones

Legend	Flood Zones
☐ MAP: City Limits	☐ Floodway
☐ MAP: UGB	■ Zone AE (100 yr)
■ MAP: Ponds	■ Zone AO (100 yr)
—— MAP: Highways	■ Zone A (100 yr)
···· MAP: RailRoad	☐ Zone X (500 yr)
—— MAP: Rivers	☐ Outside CL (100 yr)
—— MAP: Waterways	☐ Outside CL (500 yr)
···· MAP: Power Lines	
—— MAP: Contours	

Feet
0 500 1000 1500 2000

1" = 1200'
11/01/99 01.50 PM

◄ This map was drawn from the same database, but shows less detail in the city center and more in the suburbs. The shape, or relief, of the land is also presented by contour lines. Data has been combined using the GIS to calculate the areas that are most at risk from flooding.

information, along with software to draw maps and manage the data, is called a *geographic information system*, or GIS.

Once all this information has been put into the database, a range of different maps can be produced. A thematic map showing the annual sales of each shop in the mall could be drawn. A different map showing the location of all electric wires in the mall could be created. Many more maps, each one different, can be drawn on a computer screen using the GIS.

Combining Data in a GIS

It is possible to combine some of the data in the database to create some new data to be interpreted and acted on. For example, the owners of the mall might be interested in matching the cleaning schedule with the counts of numbers of shoppers in different parts of the mall. Drawing these two themes together onto one map might suggest new ideas about making the cleaners' schedules more efficient.

With GIS you can look at different combinations of data to reveal new information. And because all the data is in the computer, usually in the form of numbers, you can do calculations based on it. The shopping mall owners could use the GIS to accurately figure out the area of each shop in the mall in square feet and then get a measure of how well each shop is doing by dividing the total sales in the shop by the area. A new piece of information is created—shop sales per square foot. This new information can be stored in the GIS and mapped.

Specialized computer software is needed to run the database and to create the graphics on screen.

In addition to the data, software, and hardware, the final important thing needed to make the best use of a GIS is an experienced person. GIS can be complicated, so it is important to know exactly what kind of data is being used, and how to perform the analysis and produce the maps.

As GIS become more common in daily life, more computer scientists, geographers, and cartographers are needed to apply GIS efficiently.

Applications of GIS

A GIS can store lots of information about the positions of features and their *attributes,* or properties. It can hold very detailed information about any place in the world. It is possible, for example, to have information about the rivers and streams in a county in the same GIS as information about the county's roads, vegetation, the shape of the land, its towns and cities, parks, schools, radio transmitters, police stations, and almost any other features you can think of. This information is best thought of as a series of "layers."

The base layer is the outline map of the county. All the other information has to be held with the same coordinate system, and it could all be plotted on a computer screen at the same time if required.

But it is likely that this would be too detailed, and probably unreadable, so layers of information can be switched on and off. The layers can be viewed in different combinations, and users of GIS can examine the relationship between different themes: say, street lighting and location of auto accidents.

Some people use a GIS approach to a question without even knowing that they are doing it.

An insurance assessor, for example, may make decisions about how likely it is that floods will hit various houses in a community. In order to do this accurately, the assessor collects information such as how high above sea level each house is, how near it is to a river, how steep the slope is around the house, and what the annual rainfall is in the area. All these facts are combined to get a single percentage figure that summarizes the risk of flooding for each house. The assessor might figure out that the chance of a flood affecting a particular house in the next 10 years is 2%.

GIS would be able to help the assessor in this task a great deal. Any problem that needs information about areas of the physical world to help solve it can be made easier to deal with using GIS.

Route Planning for Emergency Services

Imagine you are in charge of a command center for emergency vehicles in a county. Ambulances, fire engines, and police cars would be under your

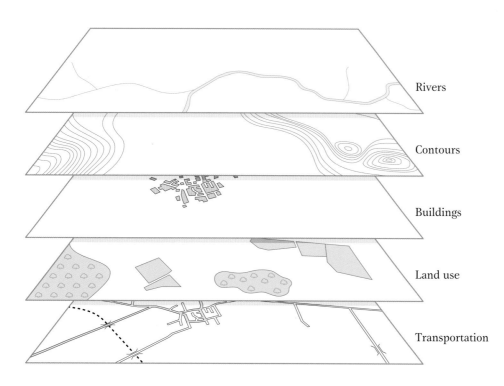

Rivers

Contours

Buildings

Land use

Transportation

◄ The information in a GIS database can be thought of as a series of layers. A large number of layers, each representing a different theme, are held in the database.

► The digital street map on the wall of this traffic control center shows the central district of Osaka in Japan. The police officers are using a GIS to manage the huge amount of rush-hour traffic in the city.

SEE ALSO: *LAYERING INFORMATION* **2:** *10–11; MAPPING ON THE WEB* **8:** *36–37*

control. The drivers of these vehicles rely on you to guide them by the quickest route to an emergency. If you had access to a GIS that held all the map information about roads and how quickly you could drive along them, you would be able to figure out the shortest or quickest route for the emergency vehicles from their current location to the position of the incident. Because a GIS routing system can be updated fairly easily, it could even include information about temporary road repair work that might slow down the response time of emergency vehicles and indicate alternative roads to be followed. GIS systems just like this are used by emergency services in many countries, saving precious time in providing assistance.

This kind of GIS information can be bought for your own car. Many databases of national road information are available to buy on a CD-ROM. They have the digitized network of roads throughout the whole country stored on them.

Figuring out School Catchment Areas

Because the GIS can calculate distances easily along a road network, it can also figure out zones. The computer can make thousands of calculations much more quickly than a human being, and so, for example, can figure out the best place to build a new school. The GIS programmer inputs information about the position (street address) of all the children in a town or section of a city. Then several alternative sites are chosen for the school.

For each trial site the total distance that all schoolchildren would need to travel is calculated by the GIS. At one site the school might be closest for perhaps 500 children, who would travel a total distance of 750 miles to and from school each day. The average distance for each pupil would therefore be 1.5 miles per day.

At another site, closer to an existing school, the new school would be the nearest one for only 300 children, and the GIS might calculate the total distance of travel per day to be 300 miles. This would be a more attractive site for a new school from the point of view of the children because each pupil would travel only 1 mile per day. But it is normally more expensive to educate a child at a smaller school than a larger one, so the planners would have to take that into account.

◄ A GIS with maps, the locations of schools, and the addresses of all the children to be collected helps the planning of routes for school buses. The location of the schools themselves is also sometimes selected using GIS databases. Such databases do not include just the addresses of schoolchildren, but also records of births to plan future school building.

► Cleaning up after an oil spill is expensive and time-consuming. A GIS can help monitor the movement of the oil slick and calculate how much would come ashore if the booms around this leaking ship failed. The GIS would include information about relevant local tides and currents. This tanker ran aground in the Straits of San Juan, Port Angeles, Washington.

GIS for the Environment

GIS is also used in the natural environment to help with many management tasks. For a forest manager, for example, it is useful to keep a record of the types of trees and their ages in every part of his or her area. This can be done with a paper map, so long as it is revised every year. But with a GIS the forest manager can plan which areas of forest should be felled next, and how much timber will be produced.

The manager will have a record of which parts of the forest are best suited to different species of tree and will know where best to site a forest fire observation tower. The GIS will also record vital wildlife habitats for rare types of bird.

GIS is sometimes used to predict environmental effects. A database with information on ocean currents, tides, the nature of the coastline, and location of sensitive sites allows a scientist to model what would happen if, for example, an oil tanker ran aground at the entrance to San Francisco Bay.

Weather forecasts rely on GIS to help store data and predict future climate patterns. Some scientists even use GIS to try to predict floods, volcanic eruptions, and landslides.

Storing Image Data in GIS

Computer progammers can store digitized data from maps in a different way than vector data. Instead of defining separate points, lines, and areas as a series of coordinates, the whole map area can instead be divided up into small cells. With this method there is a cell for every point on the map whether there is a feature there or not. If there is a feature–say, woodland or a building–the cell can be switched on; if there isn't, the cell is switched off.

Pixels

If the cells are very small, you cannot detect them with the naked eye. This technique is used in television, where the picture on the screen is made up of thousands of small cells, sometimes called "picture elements" or "pixels" for short.

With a television picture each cell is given a color, and the same principle can be applied to a map. If a pixel covers an area where there is a lake, it can be given the color blue; and if the pixel covers a line that defines a railroad, it could be given the color black. In places where there are no features, the pixels still need to be stored with a code or color indicating that they are only the "background" area.

A map that is stored in the computer database in this way is a "digital picture." This data is different from vector data–it is called *raster data*.

Using Pixels in a GIS

Although raster data can sometimes take up much more space in the computer database than vector data, it is much better for storing pictures and images. The computer software needed to handle raster data can be very different from the software for vector data. Some GIS are able to handle both

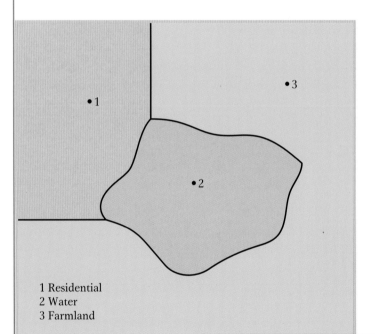

1 Residential
2 Water
3 Farmland

▲ Maps and the features on them are made up of points, lines, and areas. In a computer they can be held as "vector" information and are stored as a set of coordinates. But there is another way of storing the information that is more effective when we want to display complex map images on a screen.

1	1	1	3	3	3	3	3	3
1	1	1	3	3	3	3	3	3
1	1	2	2	2	2	3	3	3
1	1	2	2	2	2	2	3	3
1	2	2	2	2	2	3	3	3
3	3	3	2	2	2	3	3	3
3	3	3	3	2	3	3	3	3
3	3	3	3	3	3	3	3	3

◀ To show the same map on a screen, it is held as a set of small grid cells or picture elements (pixels). They are regular squares that are given a code number corresponding to their color or other attribute. This data system is called "raster." Here the number 1 represents housing (gray), 2 is the lake (blue), and 3 is farmland (green).

SEE ALSO: *MAKING SYMBOLS* **1:** *16–17; MEASURING FROM PHOTOGRAPHS* **2:** *22–25*

data types together. A popular layer in many GIS, for example, is an air photograph of the area of interest. It needs to be displayed as a raster image, built up from pixels with their color codes indicating in what shade the computer should draw them.

In some GIS it is possible to draw some vector data on top of the raster layer.

The map that is produced in this way is useful as an overview of an area. It shows, using points and lines from the vector data, man-made features such as roads, railroads, and boundaries, and natural features, such as rivers and trees. In between the lines and points, in the area that would be "background" on many normal paper maps, the raster image data shows through. It can show the gradual variation in the vegetation, agriculture, and even in the appearance of urban areas over extensive parts of the map. Every part of the map has some information to show.

Scanning Images

When aerial photographs are used as background layers in GIS and for mapmaking, they often have to be manipulated (by stretching or "warping") to make them fit properly with the other layers. And they have to be transformed from photographs into digital images. This is done by a technique known as scanning. A scanner "takes a picture" of the original photograph, which is broken down into the pixels that form the raster data. Scanners are useful devices for digitizing all types of pictures and photographs so that they can be used in GIS.

◄ A simple desktop scanner like this one is able to capture a raster picture—one made up of cells, or pixels—that can be displayed on a computer screen. All of the images in this book were scanned to make them digital images. The cartographer can make a particularly effective use of aerial photographs stored as raster data in the production of a digital map.

Raster Images from Space

Air photographs can be taken from an airplane using a specialized camera. From the air photographs measurements of features such as roads, rivers, forests, and cities are made using specialized equipment. This is the way in which maps are normally produced for large areas of the earth's surface. Today space satellites can provide the images. Instead of providing normal photographs on film or on photographic paper, modern equipment can produce photographs that have been converted into raster form suitable for handling in a computer. And these images do not have to be created by visible light.

Air photographs that have been scanned and converted into raster data can be of differing quality. The scanner can be set to record pixels that are 1/75-inch square or maybe 1/150-inch square or perhaps even 1/600-inch square. The smaller the pixel, the larger the size of the raster database, but the better the *definition* of the image. An average 17-in (40-cm) computer screen shows pictures made from pixels approximately 1/40-inch square.

The size of the pixels in an image is a measure of its *resolution*. The size of the pixels that make up the image can be compared to the size represented by a pixel "on the ground." A high-resolution air photograph might consist of pixels each of which showed 1 square foot on the ground. Each pixel can be stored in the computer as a *byte*.

Instead of taking normal photographs from the airplane and then scanning them, we can obtain the images in raster form directly by taking some form of scanner on board. A digital camera is an example of a scanner that produces raster data directly, although more complicated scanners are normally used for air photographs. They can adjust for turbulence and changes in altitude during a flight.

Such scanners can also be sent into space on satellites that orbit above the earth's surface. There are many of these satellite missions capturing raster data and sending it by radio signal back to earth. As they orbit around the earth, they are busy scanning a path across the earth's surface, sending back millions of bytes of data every day.

Image Processing

Once an image is in pixel form, it can be stored in a computer or on a disk. It can also be adjusted using computer software programs called "image-processing packages." They can modify any kind of raster data. Images from satellites, from scanned air photographs, and from raster layers in a GIS can all be modified.

There are many jobs that an image-processing package can perform. It is possible, for example, to stretch and distort raster data to make it match up to the rest of the data in a GIS. Satellite images may not have been taken looking straight down onto the part of the earth being mapped, but at an angle instead. A map shows that straight-down view, so if the image and the map are to be combined, the image has to be adjusted to fit the map. This process is called "registration" or "warping," and image-processing software can do it. Registration gives the image coordinates that can be read using the software in the same way that the grid on a map is used.

One of the main reasons for using image-processing software is to detect details that the human eye finds difficult to pick out. The software can, for example, find all the straight lines on an image. So a satellite image can be used to automatically pick out all the roads in an area. It is also easy for the software to select all areas that look the same. A computer

▶ This picture of Venice, Italy, was taken by a scanner on board an orbiting satellite. It is a raster image made up of pixels that have a resolution of 1 meter on the ground. This means that it is possible to see quite easily very small features such as the boats in the canals, even in an image taken from 425 miles (680 km) above the earth.

SEE ALSO: *PHOTOGRAPHS AND MAPS* **1**: *12–13; MEASURING FROM PHOTOGRAPHS* **2**: *22–25*

operator could pick out one pixel that is known to be forest and ask the software to find every other pixel with the same reference number (see diagram on page 16). The result is an automatically created forest map. The image-processing package can then count up the number of forest pixels and figure out the total area of forest.

Seeing beyond Visible Light

The pictures taken using a camera in an airplane will normally show part of the earth as it is seen in the daylight. Such cameras can be loaded with normal color film (sometimes black-and-white film is still used) that produces a picture as our eyes see it. The film is sensitive to visible light, the light that we see, and is called *panchromatic* film. What the film senses is light that comes from the sun and is reflected from features on the earth's surface. Obviously, the sun's light reflects as a green color from leaves and grass, but reflects as a brown or orange color from sand and desert, and that is what panchromatic film records.

But the visible light waves that are captured by such panchromatic film are only part of the range of radiation that exists. This wide range of waves is called the "spectrum." Visible light is a form of radiation: Radio waves, ultraviolet rays, infrared light, and x-rays are also part of the spectrum.

Images from different parts of the spectrum provide different information. For example, infrared radiation images highlight water features. Infrared light is absorbed almost completely by water, so it appears black on infrared film. Infrared can also be used to show vegetation, such as trees, that have disease: Healthy trees reflect more infrared, while dying trees absorb it.

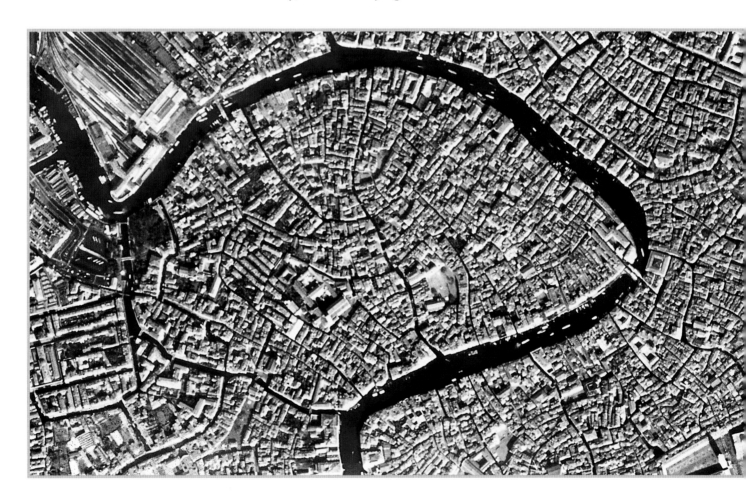

Extent of the Electromagnetic Spectrum

The light that we see everyday from the sun or a light bulb takes up just a small part of the electromagnetic spectrum. Features on the earth reflect electro-magnetic waves at different places on the spectrum in different ways, so that new ways of mapping the earth become possible. Even deep space has its own spectral signature. Gamma rays, x-rays, and radio waves detect-ed on earth arriving from space are the clues astronomers use in their continuing attempts to map the universe.

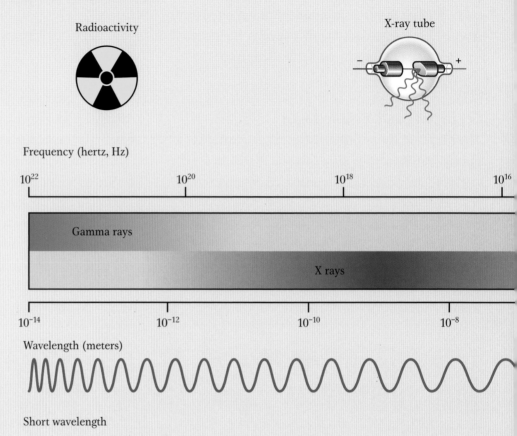

Spectral Signatures

Environmental scientists have noticed that many features on the earth's surface reflect different parts of the spectrum in different ways. The full pattern of *reflectance* of features at different parts of the spectrum is called the spectral signature. The spectral signature of some types of rock, for example, those with high iron content, differs from those rocks with a high aluminum content; wet soil reflects differently than dry soil; birch trees reflect with a different spectral signature than pine trees.

The scanners on board satellites are able to sense reflectance in many different parts of the spectrum, which helps in mapping rock types, soil classification, vegetation species, and other natural features.

The images can also be used to pick up man-made features. Roads, for example, reflect radiation differently than gardens.

Most of the satellite missions have been launched with spectral scanners designed to identify specific features. Some satellites are used to look at weather patterns on the earth's surface; others concentrate on the oceans and map currents and waves. Some missions examine the growth of deserts; others show how cities are expanding across the world.

Advantages of Satellite Data

If we want to use satellite images to create maps of desert growth or urban expansion, we can capture data from more than one moment in time. Then we

SEE ALSO: *THE EARTH FROM SPACE* **1**: *6–7; MODERN GEOLOGICAL MAPPING* **8**: *28–29*

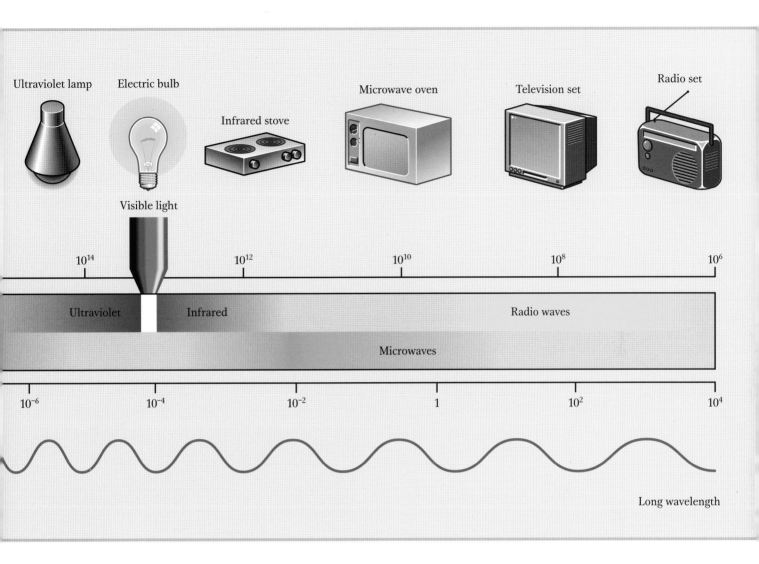

Ultraviolet lamp Electric bulb Infrared stove Microwave oven Television set Radio set

Visible light

10^{14} 10^{12} 10^{10} 10^8 10^6

Ultraviolet Infrared Radio waves

Microwaves

10^{-6} 10^{-4} 10^{-2} 1 10^2 10^4

Long wavelength

can create a map showing the difference between the earlier size of the desert or city and the up-to-date one. Using satellite images of the same area of the earth taken at different times, we can examine the effect of global warming and the melting of the ice at the North and South Poles or the increasing destruction of the rain forests. Because the scanners are on unmanned satellites and can last up to 20 years in orbit, they are a cheap way of obtaining images of the earth's surface for mapping and environmental monitoring.

Producing images from different parts of the spectrum means that satellite scanners can detect and map many different types of features. All the images sent back from satellites to earth are already in digital raster form. So we can include the images in geographical information systems for visual display. In addition, the data can be processed using image-processing software packages, and extra information can be obtained from it.

Improving Resolution of Satellite Images

One of the major problems with satellite data is its *resolution*. Because the satellites orbit high above the earth's surface, the size of the pixels "on the ground" is usually quite large. This means that the images can look "fuzzy," and they cannot be used to identify small features on the earth's surface. They are "low-resolution" images. However, there are secret spy satellites that carry precision telescopes in space

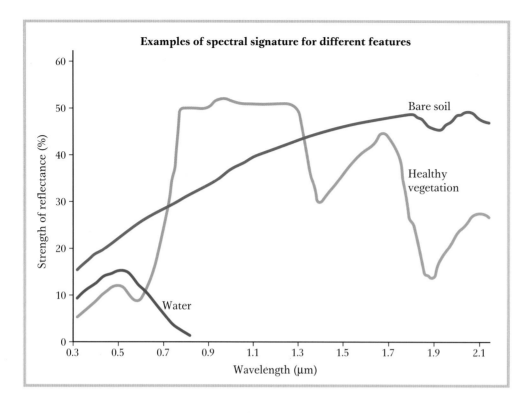

Examples of spectral signature for different features

Strength of reflectance (%)

Wavelength (μm)

Bare soil

Healthy vegetation

Water

◄ This diagram covers that part of the spectrum from blue light on the left with a wavelength of 0.3μm, or 0.3 micrometers, to red light in the middle (1.0 μm) and the infrared waves (up to 2.0μm). A micrometer is one millionth of a meter. Different features on the earth reflect different electromagnetic waves in varying amounts.

▼ Reflectance across the visible part of the spectrum for Africa, from images taken by the Landsat Thematic Mapper satellite.

looking back down to earth. They can can find small objects such as people. Such satellites produce "high-resolution" images.

The images beaming back to earth from remote sensing satellites are not as high-resolution as the spy satellite. But the resolution has improved since the first of these satellites was launched in the early 1970s. The first Landsat mission went into orbit in 1972, and the images sent back had a pixel resolution of about 80 meters on the ground. These images were used to look at environmental conditions over large areas on the earth for the first time. Scientists examined the effect of logging in tropical rain forests and examined coastal waters to detect pollution. The instruments on board could sense infrared light as well as visible light, and so they were good at monitoring vegetation and the natural environment. But because of the low resolution it was not possible to make accurate maps from these images.

Since the first satellite missions many more have followed, and most have provided images with much higher resolution. The IKONOS satellite, for example,

SEE ALSO: *THE GLOBAL POSITIONING SYSTEM* **4:** *30–33;* *MAPPING THE ENEMY* **6:** *28–29*

launched in 1999, can beam back pictures with a pixel size of 1 meter. These images are black-and-white, but on them we can clearly see small buildings. Cartographers are pleased to be able to get these images from satellites because in the past they would have needed to plan complicated and time-consuming airplane operations to take such photographs. Today pictures from space can provide the same information as pictures taken from airplanes.

As with air photographs, it is necessary to manipulate the images before accurate maps can be made using them. Measurements can only be made and positions calculated after the images have been twisted into the right shape to be registered with other map information. Since the images are held in raster form, this is fairly easy to do. Manipulation of the data can also bring out details. The image on the right shows a radar view of the Great Wall of China created by merging four separate images taken at slightly different radar wavelengths. Vegetation has been colored red and water black.

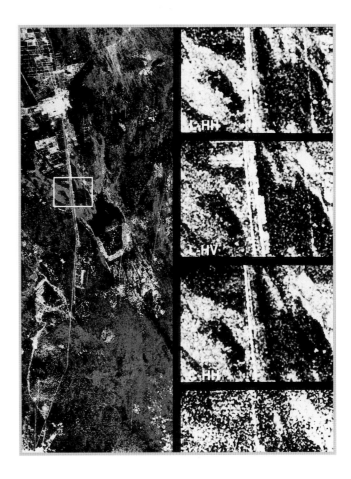

▲ Even a slight variation in the spectral wavelength recorded can improve the quality of the information received, as in these pictures of the Great Wall of China. Longer wavelength radar is good for "seeing" through clouds. The four separate images are all of the highlighted rectangle to the left.

◄ Deforestation is clearly shown in this Landsat view of Rondonia, Brazil. The jungle, shown in red, is being cleared on a huge scale by farmers burning the trees (blue areas).

Mapping the Stars and Planets

We understand that all the features we see on maps are located on the surface of a globe, the earth. All other bodies in our Solar System are roughly spherical and can be mapped in the same way–if we can record their surfaces. But how do we map the positions of the stars in space? There is no "surface" to map.

The environment on other planets is very different from earth, so it is difficult to use exactly the same mapping techniques. There is no concept of sea level anywhere else, so how do we measure the heights of mountains on Mars? The answer is to take the lowest point we can find and the highest mountain, then *layer tint* the map accordingly. How can we get images of the surface of Venus when it is always covered with clouds? Through satellite radar.

If the planet or moon is not a true sphere, which is true for most of Jupiter's moons, how can we use map projections to create a flat paper map? We compromise: After all, the earth is not a true sphere either.

Telescopes have been used in the past to examine the moon, Venus, and Mars, our closest heavenly bodies (although telescopes are useless for

seeing through the thick clouds around Venus). For planetary mapping beyond this, techniques rely on satellite-based images sent back as digital raster pictures to earth. They are collected using radar, television cameras, and other imaging equipment.

Mapping the Night Sky

When we look at ways of mapping outer space, we come across a range of difficulties. The universe is not a flat or a familiar globe shape, so it is tricky to come up with a method for locating features. Latitude and longitude, or coordinates, cannot be used in the same way as they are on the surface of the earth. In the vastness of the universe what

▶ This color-coded map of Mars uses the same techniques as earth mapping to display the height of the mountains on the "red planet." Millions of heights were obtained from an altimeter (height-measuring instrument) orbiting Mars. The large mountain to the upper left of this image is *Olympus Mons*, the largest volcano in our Solar System.

▲ This three dimensional view of a 3-mile (5-km) high volcano on the surface of Venus is a combination of radar images and altimeter data. Venus is covered with cloud and is never as clear as this; the image has been colored to highlight lava flows.

◄ An astronomer gazes at the night sky dominated by the Milky Way, our own galaxy. Only in remote parts of the earth, such as here in the Superstition Mountains of Arizona, does it become dark and clear enough for us to be able to map the faintest stars.

should we use as a "zero point" from which all measurements will be taken? The objects in the universe that we may want to measure and plot, and perhaps use as zero points of reference, such as galaxies and *black holes*, are either too large and three-dimensional or else cannot be sensed accurately enough because they are not light enough or are too far away.

The main solution to creating maps of the sky is to imagine a large globe with the earth at its center. It is called the *celestial globe*. The locations of all the visible comets, planets, stars, and galaxies can be plotted on the inside of that globe. The distance of these objects away from the earth is ignored using this method. All that is recorded is the position of these objects as they appear from the earth. Even though the objects are plotted on the inside of the globe (rather than the outside, which is what is done when maps are made of the earth), we can still

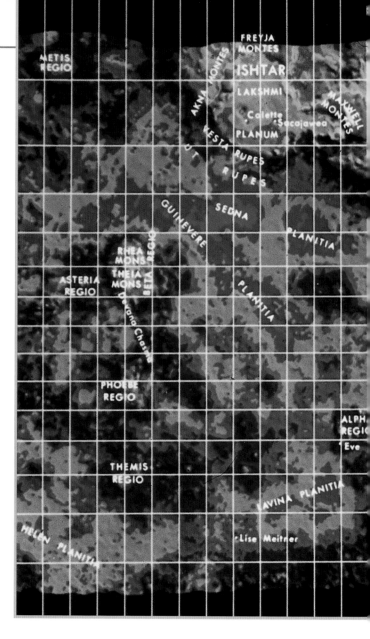

▼ Mission Control at the time of Voyager 1's encounter with Saturn. To control a space mission that travels millions of miles into the unknown, the position of the spacecraft and accurate time must be constantly recorded. Position and time: the key data for all earthly navigators in history as well.

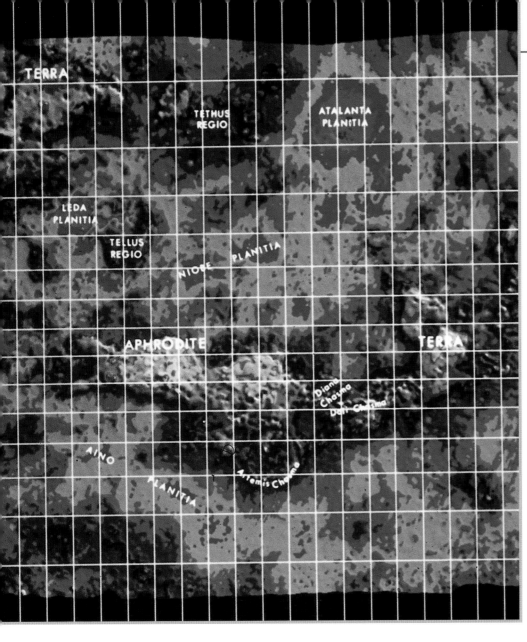

TERRA

TETHUS REGIO

ATALANTA PLANITIA

LEDA PLANITIA

TELLUS REGIO

NTIOBE PLANITIA

APHRODITE

TERRA

Diana Chasma

Dali Chasma

AINO

PLANITIA

Artemis Chasma

◄ A topographic map of the surface of Venus shown on a map projection. This projection is similar to Mercator's: It is not only when mapping the earth that we need map projections to show a spherical body on a flat piece of paper. The problem is the same for all planets.

▼ Part of a map of the "celestial globe." Instead of latitude and longitude, declination (−40°, −30° and −20°) and right ascension (measured in hours, 12, 13, and 14) are shown. This section of the sky contains the Centaurus *constellation*. Just like a terrestrial map, certain features−certain stars−are considered important enough to be named; others are not.

create a reference system, like latitude and longitude, to locate them.

The system is very similar to the earth's location system. There are "celestial poles," which are the points on the celestial globe directly above the earth's poles, and there is a "celestial equator" drawn around the celestial globe above the earth's equator. Instead of using latitude and longitude to position features on the inside of the celestial globe, the terms used are "declination" and "right ascension."

The major problem is that the pattern of stars and planets in the sky is constantly changing. It is important that every map of the night sky indicate the time of day and the day of the year at which it is a true picture.

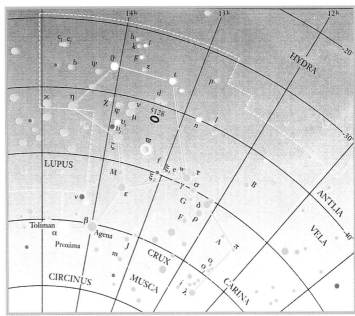

SEE ALSO: *LATITUDE, LONGITUDE, AND POSITIONING* **2:** 26–29; *FINDING YOUR WAY BY THE STARS* **4:** 6–7

Modern Geological Mapping

The earth beneath our feet is hidden from us, although the shapes we see on the earth's surface depend on the complex geology of the first few miles of solid rock. We can only be absolutely sure what is under there by caving or tunneling, mining, and digging under the surface. Mankind has been doing that for centuries. But modern instruments can give us useful clues without all the hard work.

There is a long tradition of making maps of the solid rock beneath our feet. This has been done in order to find and mine the rich resources of the earth. Coal, gold, oil and many other products are taken from areas that have been mapped by geologists over the last two centuries.

Geological mapping can be carried out using a number of techniques. The earliest geologists interpreted rock layers by looking at the shape of the surface of the earth. Later methods involved scientific examination of soil samples and trial drilling. Following the invention of the airplane, exploration geologists used air photographs both to make maps and to interpret the patterns of the earth's surface. They looked for large geological structures such as fault lines and rock basins, which might not be obvious from ground level.

Sometimes it is possible to predict the existence of certain minerals in the ground by looking at the vegetation types shown on the photographs. Some species of tree, for example, grow faster and healthier on soil with a high concentration of manganese than on soil containing a large amount of some other minerals (such as aluminum).

There can be other instruments on board

◄ A satellite radar "contour map" of the results of a California earthquake. By combining the "before" and "after" images, each color band shows a 4-inch (10-cm) movement in the earth's surface.

▲ This image of the basin of the Bighorn River in Wyoming, taken from the Landsat Thematic Mapper satellite mission, has been color-coded to emphasize the banded rock formations.

SEE ALSO: *MAPPING FEATURES BELOW THE SURFACE* **6:** *16–17* airplanes as well as cameras. A magnetometer, for example, is a device sensitive to magnetic variation in the earth's surface over which it flies. It can find iron ore and other magnetic minerals.

Even satellite images can be used in exploration for minerals. The reflectance of different minerals (their "spectral signatures," see page 20) can reveal outcrops of valuable resources worth mining for. Image-processing techniques can be used to detect and zoom into likely areas of mineral wealth. In remote parts of the world, such as Siberia in Russia or central Australia, it is often much cheaper to look at satellite images than to send geologists out to explore and map on the ground.

Ground Penetrating Radar

Other people are interested in what is underground apart from geologists looking for minerals. The technology of ground-penetrating radar allows images to be captured of solid objects buried 10 or 12 feet down.

Once a site has been cleared of vegetation and other surface features, a transmitting antenna is placed on, or into, the ground. A radio signal sent into the ground reflects in different ways from different materials. The soil itself conducts the signal better or worse depending on its type and the amount of moisture in it. The most obvious features picked up are boundaries between soil and metal, and disturbed or undisturbed ground.

Archaeologists, therefore, use ground-penetrating radar to detect human activity that has long since been buried. Burial sites, ancient roadways, and outlines of buildings can all be picked up before undertaking archaeological digs.

Other workers who dig into the earth, for example, maintenance engineers trying to reach damaged wires and pipes, find underground radar maps useful. It is often difficult to precisely locate these *utilities*, and accurate radar information helps keep roadwork and disruption to a minimum.

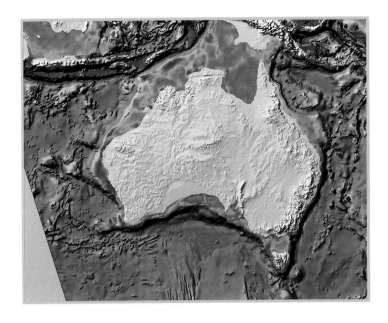

▲ Measuring height and sea depth using satellite altimeters allows us to build up a picture of the shape of the earth and to locate the edges of the "plates" on the earth's surface, where volcanoes are found and earthquakes are most likely to happen. The Java Trench (upper left here) is the boundary between the Asian and the Australian plates.

▼ Magnetic map of a burial mound. Created in 600 A.D., the bear-shaped mound is at the Effigy Mounds National Monument, Iowa. The disturbance of the ground and the creation of the mound by native tribes have led to variation in the magnetic properties below the surface. See Volume 6, page 16 for the raw data from which this map was made.

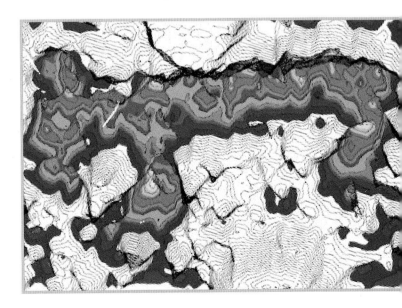

Mapping the Microscopic and Submicroscopic

Most maps show large areas, such as your neighborhood or even a whole country. The map represents a larger area than itself. But the scale can be reversed, and things smaller than the map can be the subject.

Maps are just as useful for describing very small objects and presenting information about them. Even objects viewed through a microscope can be positioned to create a map. Scientists use the same techniques used in making landscape maps to map the microscopic surfaces of metal, say, or a

computer chip. Contours show the shape of all the small depressions and the rough surface; and any minute cracks, which are sometimes found in weak metal, can be detected. Such maps are used for quality control in precision engineering.

Mapping the Human Genome

Modeling of molecules–showing how atoms combine with each other–is a kind of three-dimensional mapping. This kind of mapping is being used to record the human genome. The genome is the combined "set of instructions," or "blueprint," that is

▼ A computer-generated view of DNA. The blue nitrogen, the yellow carbon and phosphorus, and the red oxygen atoms are joined by cross-linked *nucleotide bases*. This is not a photograph of DNA: It is a visual representation that can be read like a map.

▶ This image of some individual genes was taken by an electron microscope at a magnification of nearly 30,000 times. The strands of DNA have joined in a particular pattern to form genes that have been colored by a computer in this view.

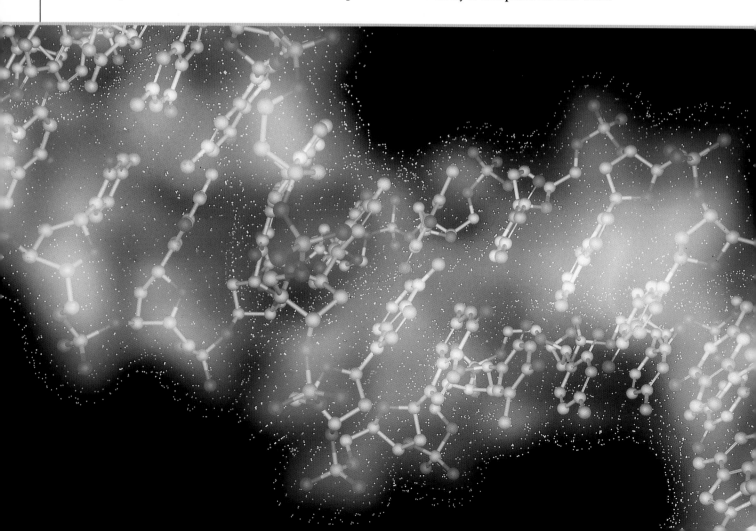

in the nucleus of every cell in the human body. The human genome is itself made up of at least 30,000 genes (some say 80,000). These genes together tell cells how to split to reproduce themselves, organize, and come together to create a human being.

Like maps of the world, maps of the genome are made at different scales. The largest scale map, the most detailed, shows *DNA* and its components. The deoxyribonucleic acid (DNA) threads are composed of two strands of molecules connected by "bases," as shown in the image on page 30. The DNA strands have sets of repeated sequences of bases along their length. These sequences are the genes, which carry all our characteristics inherited from our parents. Identifying the genes allows us to predict potential genetic illnesses and disabilities. A smaller-scale

map—one that shows less detail—represents the way in which the genes together build up into *chromosomes*, of which each cell nucleus has 46. Chromosomes are relatively large: They are made up of 3 billion DNA base pairs! They can actually be seen under a light microscope.

Using high-magnification electron microscopes, geneticists can map the location of the DNA threads along the chromosomes.

Learning to Read the Map

The ultimate aim is to create a map of the whole human genome. It is the complete DNA sequence for the whole of each chromosome. This is a very complex set of molecules to display, and digital cartographic methjods are one of the tools helping give us pictures of the building blocks of human life.

We still have much to learn about how cells, chromosomes, genes, and DNA combine. Once the map is complete, then the work begins of interpreting it. Apart from the incredibly large numbers of base pairs in DNA, another difficulty is that not all of the DNA molecule forms genes. Imagine mapping a huge forest in great detail and then finding out that many of the trees were dummies!

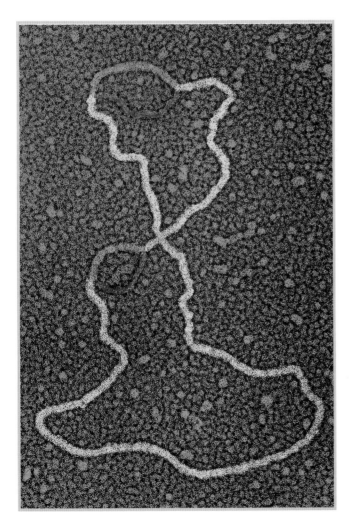

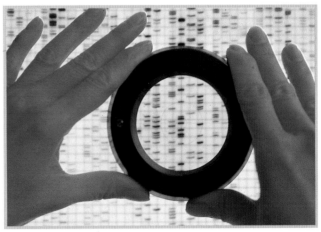

▲ The sequence of DNA patterns can be coded and brought together into a map of the whole human genome. This plot of the elements of one gene shows all the DNA sequences. It is being digitized.

SEE ALSO: *MAPS OF INVISIBLE THINGS* **1:** *34–35; DIGITAL MAPPING* **8:** *6–7*

Visualization

Maps are really good tools for "visualizing" the earth. The human eye and brain cannot deal with too much complex information, and maps simplify the picture of the real world. A map can give a clearer explanation than a list of statistics, and modern computers provide new ways of visualizing information.

Summarizing Data

Any list of connected numbers is much better shown as a picture of some kind. A set of daily temperature values over a month or year, the value of shares on the stock exchange, or the population density of a number of countries can be plotted onto a graph. The conversion of numbers, facts, and positions into graphs, charts, and maps is called "visualization."

Today scientists and other people have to store and handle much more information than they ever used to. Scientific experiments can produce huge amounts of data and statistics, far more than scientists could have gathered together before computers. *Meteorologists*, for example, record thousands of daily readings of temperature, humidity, and pressure. Some scientists rely on equipment that is not operated by a human being but is switched on and sends back information to their office all the time. There are instruments placed on the sides of volcanoes and at potential earthquake sites to check ground movement 24 hours a day. Mapping scientists also use unmanned instruments sending back information. The remote sensing satellites are constantly beaming back thousands of raster images.

All this information needs to be recorded and analyzed, and one of the best ways of bringing it together and making some sense of it is to visualize it. When the information is about the earth or about people spread over a large area like a city or nation, a map is the best visualization tool.

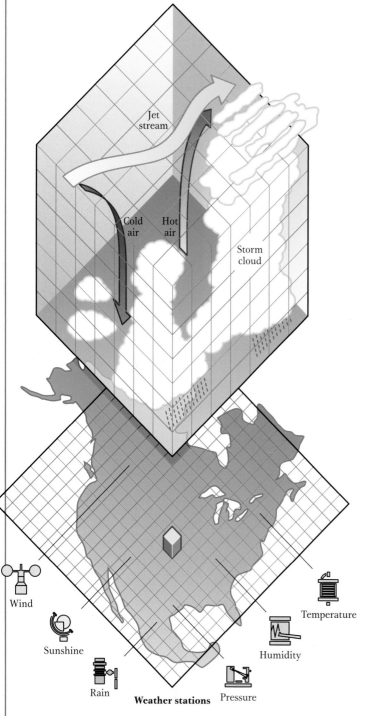

Wind
Sunshine
Rain
Jet stream
Cold air
Hot air
Storm cloud
Temperature
Humidity
Pressure
Weather stations

◀ Many different weather observations by different instruments provide the data for this model of the weather in part of the atmosphere over the Midwest. The three-dimensional diagram is a good summary of the weather conditions. If further observations were added (for the days before and after), a "movie" could be created in a computer showing changes over a period of time. And the computer can analyze the patterns to predict the coming weather.

SEE ALSO: *THE END FOR THE PAPER AIR CHART* **4**: 36–37; *VIRTUAL ENVIRONMENTS* **8**: 34–35

New Uses for Cartographic Skills

Skilled cartographers make maps that show just the right amount of information: They are not too detailed and not too simple. Visualization of data in any form, not just as a map–as a graph for example, or a pie chart or *pictogram*–demands exactly the same skills. Information is brought together from different sources and illustrated, just as the cartographer collects data from many different places and summarizes that data in visual form.

So the skills of the cartographer are used today to handle information that is not only about the earth. The new possibilities for visualization that computers provide and their ability to process large amounts of information have not made cartographers jobless! In fact, cartographic skills have become even more important with so much more information available to be mapped.

Maps can carry more information than ever before. For example, maps can be made showing change over time–like the spread of disease or the path of a hurricane. The map is made into a moving image on a computer screen. Also, maps are not restricted any more to the straight-down view. It has always been difficult to show the height of mountains using a flat map. But by creating a computer model that the map reader can fly around as in a simulator, he or she can get a more accurate impression of the landscape. Maps are moving away from being two-dimensional (flat) and static (just one image) to being three-dimensional and dynamic.

▼ This map summarizes a large amount of data that, if it was presented only as a list of statistics, would be very difficult to understand. The average summer temperature across the U.S. is mapped by the Spatial Climate Analysis Service, Oregon State University.

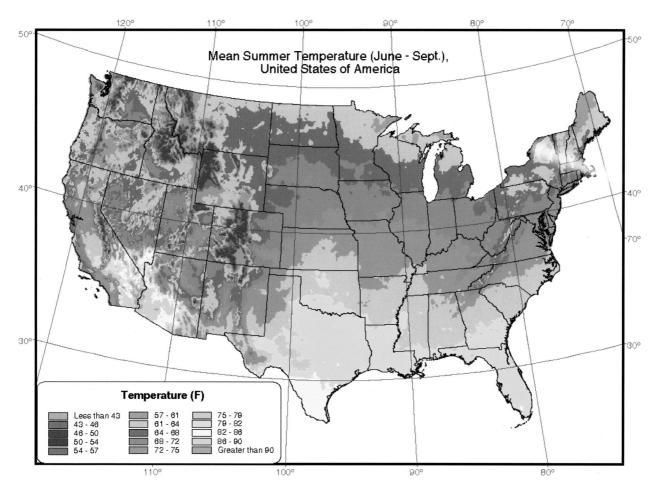

Mean Summer Temperature (June - Sept.), United States of America

Temperature (F)

Less than 43	57 - 61	75 - 79
43 - 46	61 - 64	79 - 82
46 - 50	64 - 68	82 - 86
50 - 54	68 - 72	86 - 90
54 - 57	72 - 75	Greater than 90

Virtual Environments

Most people have tried computer games in arcades or on a PC that require the player to navigate through a make-believe world, fighting off dragons (or mutants) or searching for treasure. Cartographic techniques are used to produce those worlds, and not all "make-believe" worlds are created just for fun.

Multiuser dungeons (or MUDs) are examples of these games where you can compete with other players even over the Internet. Some of these contests are set in the future, and you are able to rush around a landscape or a fictional city on a vehicle controlled by your game pad. Driving and flight simulation games have detailed pictures of landscapes. Many of them are imaginary; others are representations of the real world.

Since maps are also representations of the real world, there is a link between the digital pictures in your computer game and the science of cartography.

Some cartographers today find that in their daily work they have to create "virtual environments"–representations of landscapes made by computers–for a range of uses, including games.

Creating virtual environments can rely on existing maps: They need to be digitized (see page 6) and improved by adding height information and further detail. Sometimes the maps are combined with photographs to give a more realistic view of the landscape. For many of the uses of virtual environments the aim of the designer is to make them look as realistic as possible. In some cases, especially in MUDs, the environment can have artificial people (called avatars) walking around it and interacting with you.

This is usually a different aim than that of traditional cartographers. Their goal is to "generalize" the real world to achieve a clear map that only has the most important information on it. They filter out the complex and less vital detail.

◀ The planetarium at Jodrell Bank radio observatory, near Manchester, England. Planetariums are one of the earliest examples of virtual environments. The view of the night sky can be changed to show how stars appear in different seasons and from different locations.

▶ Interior of a cockpit flight simulator for the Boeing 737-300 airliner. The to-scale view of the urban airport at dusk is computer-generated.

SEE ALSO: *GENERALIZATION* **1**: *14–15*; *THE END FOR THE PAPER AIR CHART* **4**: *36–37*

Not Just for Entertainment

In addition to being an important part of computer games, virtual environments are used for serious scientific work. They can simulate a journey through a dangerous area, such as a nuclear power plant or under the sea, in order to minimize risk by training operators for the real thing or even to make the actual journey unnecessary. They are essential to train airplane pilots. The virtual airport in the picture below left is a cartographic creation made to look as realistic as possible but based on mapping projection and accurate use of scale.

Virtual environments enable students to interact with historical figures in ancient landscapes. Using some technologies, it is possible for a group of people to share such experiences. If you have ever been in a *planetarium*, you have been exposed with others to an early example of a virtual environment.

How Real?

According to the level of realism required, it may be necessary to add sounds. Depending on the type of technology used, it may also be possible to add forces to objects, like mass and gravity.

Virtual environments of landscapes sometimes need a full representation of what can be experienced by the senses, including vision, hearing, and balance. This representation can include the true visual location of features, such as buildings and rivers, you can't see around corners or in the dark or clouds that may obscure your view. It can indicate how hard or soft features would be if someone navigating through the environment was to "bump" against them or "fall" into them.

The ways vary in which these virtual environments are presented. They can be presented simply on the screen of a normal computer and navigated through using a mouse or game pad. A flight simulator for training pilots, however, needs to have an accurate reconstruction of a cockpit, with the right seats, windows, control panel, and instruments. In addition, the whole cockpit structure usually moves around to give the sensation of true flight.

One of the uses of virtual environments is to test something that all mapmakers are always thinking about: How much information can the viewer, or map reader, take in? If maps are too complex, they become unreadable; if the flight simulator is too difficult, the cockpit design must be changed.

▲ The officer wearing a virtual reality helmet can "pick up" circles representing landing zones or military targets and place them on the virtual battlefield.

Mapping on the Web

The most important method of communicating information today is the Internet, the huge number of computers and connections that span the world. The World Wide Web (or just the "Web") is the way in which the Internet is used to transfer knowledge and data from one computer to another. It is used for sending messages, for entertainment, for information and news, for shopping and commerce, and also for scientific reasons.

As well as text, the Web is a good way of sending photographs, images, and other pictures because the software used is able to handle them effectively. Maps are also easy to send over the Web, and many people rely on "web maps" to find locations and plan routes.

Interaction with Web Maps

Web maps can be a bit like maps on paper or in atlases. A map can be scanned in and be put alongside text on a web page displayed on the computer screen. This map is just a copy, perhaps shown to point out the position of a store or office. But it is possible to add something more dynamic and exciting for the viewer. It might be useful to have a flashing symbol at the store location. You couldn't put this on a paper map, but a computer map on the Web is able to do it. And such straightforward visual additions are only the very simplest kind of improvement that can be made to the old-style map.

You might like to see a closer view of the position of the store, and so a "zoom" facility would be useful. It lets you magnify the immediate area around the location.

It is also possible to "pan" around the map, moving beyond the edges of what is on the screen to show the area some distance away from the store. That is how route-planning software shows the journey along the highway from your house to another location you select. Such route planning can also be done over the Web.

The complicated manipulation of map information that a geographic information system can perform is also available over the Web. Maps can have layers switched on and off. Calculations can be made of areas and distances. Questions can be asked about features shown on the map. And the maps can be quickly updated.

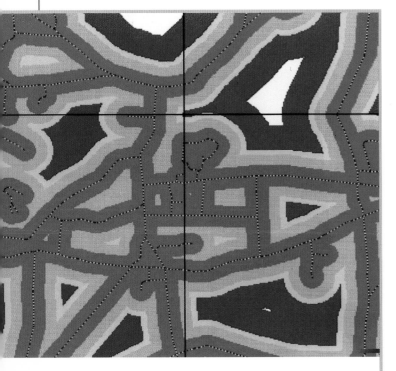

72° 32' 30.27" W (−72.5417) 41° 55' 23.76" N (41.9233)
703844   m   4643966   m
9723   univ   5434   univ
Grid Reference   18TYB 384443966

well	PROXIMITY TO WELLS	.5	km
circ	PROXIMITY TO POLLUTION	1	km
road	CORRIDORS FROM ROADS	.5	km
slop	COMPOSITE SLOPE	0	%

◄ Scientists and researchers can get access to mapping information on the Web in a fraction of the time it used to take before the exchange of ideas over the Internet. This map is part of a GIS database that analyzes the risks of pollution of the water supply over an area of land. The Web map reader can position the "crosshair" pointer—the two dark lines—anywhere on the map and obtain a readout (below) of latitude, longitude, closeness to wells, and other information.

SEE ALSO: *MAP MATERIALS THROUGH HISTORY* 1: *18–19; CITY TOURIST GUIDES* 7: *36–37*

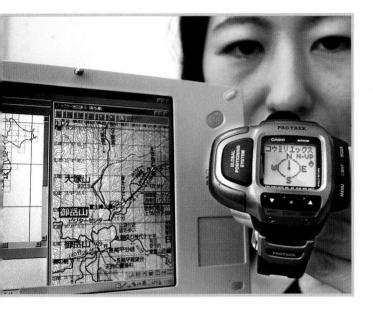

▲ This GPS wristwatch, called the "Satellite Navi PRT-2GP," was designed by the Japanese company Casio Computer. It not only gives the wearer's location but can also link to a computer to show that location on a map

▼ This in-car map is continually updated through a mobile phone connection to the Internet. The map face changes as the driver moves toward the edge of the mapped area, recentering the display and zooming into the fine detail if necessary.

Maps through Mobiles

Many of the connections of the Internet are not through wires or telephone lines, but by mobile communications. Some mobile phones are able to use the Web and receive and send information. Modern mobile phones also have sophisticated screens that can draw graphical information. So it is possible to call up from a mobile phone and receive a map drawn on the screen.

Imagine a businessman visiting a city that is new to him. He has already called ahead from the mobile phone on the airplane to book a rental car. Sitting in the driver's seat, he uses his own phone to call up a route-planning service to find the way from the airport to the client he has to visit. The screen on the mobile draws a simple map, and he also receives instructions ("turn left out of the airport onto Interstate 395, take the 3rd exit") through the phone. After his meeting he is staying at a city center hotel, but wants to find the nearest Italian restaurant. This time the mobile phone connects to a Web page listing the possible restaurants, and a map shows their locations.

The Mapmaking Rules Do Not Change

As more and more cartographers are asked to provide maps and data for Web-linked computers and phones, they still need to keep in mind the cartographic rules. Mapmakers collect information about places and features on the earth. They combine this information with data from various sources depending on the reason for the map. They design a good presentation of the information that is easy to read and shows what the map reader wants to see. Accuracy is vital.

Although maps are presented in very different ways today, cartographers still use the same guidelines as Ptolemy, Idrisi, Mercator, and Captain Cook did when they were making maps centuries ago. Or at least they should: Disorganized information is not really information at all.

Glossary

Words in *italics* have their own entries in the glossary

Aerial photograph (or air photograph) – a photograph looking straight down at the earth, taken from an airplane

Altimeter – on earth an instrument that measures height above sea level, usually put in an aircraft; in space an instrument that can record the height of points on a planet's surface above or below a selected zero position

Astronomy – the scientific study of celestial bodies (planets and stars) and of the universe as a whole. People who do this are called astronomers

Attribute – a particular characteristic of an object or feature shown on a map, such as the pollution in a lake or the name of a building

Avatars – representations of people in computer *virtual environments*, with characteristics that govern their interaction with the user

Black hole – an object in the universe that is so dense and large that its immensely strong gravity even sucks in radiation such as light. Because of this black holes cannot be seen, but they can be located by the complete lack of radiation from them

Byte – the basic storage unit of data in a computer

Catchment area – the area from which people are allocated to a particular school, hospital, or other public body

CD-ROM – Compact Disk-Read Only Memory; a method of storing digital information on a plastic disk that can be read by a computer

Celestial globe – a model of the imaginary sphere enclosing the universe, with the earth at the center, that maps the relative position of the planets, stars, and *constellations* as they appear to us in the skies

Chromosomes – the rod-shaped structures in a cell nucleus made up of the genes that pass on characteristics from one generation to the next. The number of chromosomes is the same in every cell, but varies from one species of plant or animal to the next

Computer graphics – how graphical features, such as maps, are displayed and manipulated on the screen of a computer

Constellation – a group of fixed stars in the night sky appearing to form a group. Usually named with reference to the shape the group takes, for example, the Big Dipper

Contour – an imaginary line connecting places in the landscape that are at equal height above (or below) sea level. The distance of contour lines from each other on a map shows how steeply or gradually land rises

Coordinates – the pair of values that define a position on a graph or on a map with a coordinate system (such as latitude and longitude). On a map the coordinates "55ºN 45ºE" indicate a position of 55 degrees north of latitude, 45 degrees east of longitude

Customizing – changing something according to personal specifications or preference

Database – a collection of facts, measurements, or information stored in a digital form

Definition – the visual clarity of an image

Digitizing – the task of converting information and images, such as maps, into the form of numbers that can be stored in a computer

Digitizing tablet – a flat table on which a map is fixed and over which a mouse or other pointer is placed that can sense and record the *coordinates* of features on the map

DNA (deoxyribonucleic acid) – an extremely long molecule that is the main component of *chromosomes* and is the material that transfers genetic characteristics in all life

Dynamic maps – computerized maps that have some element that allows for movement or animation and so can show change over time. Such maps need specialized software for display

Equator – an imaginary line running around the earth at equal distance from the North and South Poles. It is the line at 0 degrees *latitude*

Geographic information system (GIS) – a computer-based digital store of geographic information about an area, which can be consulted and analyzed

Geology – the study of the rocks under the earth's surface and their structure

Global positioning system (GPS) – a system of 24 satellites orbiting the earth and sending out highly accurate radio signals indicating where they are; a GPS receiver held by someone on the earth can interpret the signals and calculate the receiver's position on earth

GPS receiver – *see* Global positioning system

Human genome – the full set of *chromosomes* that together define all the characteristics that human beings inherit from their parents

Idrisi, ash-Sharif al- (1100–1165 or 1166) – Arab geographer who worked for much of his life for the king of Sicily. He created a world map divided into sections by *longitude*, and a huge geographical book describing the known world, using accounts from travelers plus ancient Greek and Arab texts. Arab scholars like Idrisi retained ancient Greek learning that was lost in western Europe for centuries

Image processing – the modification of photographs or satellite images by computer software

Infrared – a part of the spectrum close to red, but detected by the senses as heat, rather than light; infrared radiation is not visible to the eye but can be recorded by some sensors

Internet – the network of interconnected computers throughout the world linked by wires and satellites and running software to allow them to communicate with each other

Latitude – the line joining places of equal angular distance from the center of the earth in a north-south direction. The equator is zero degrees latitude, the poles are at 90 degrees latitude north and south

Layer tinting – showing height of mountains and hills on a map using bands of color to define zones where the land is between two height measurements (between 100 and 250 meters above sea level, for example)

Longitude – a line connecting places of equal angular distance from the center of the earth, measured in degrees east or west of the Prime Meridian, which is at 0 degrees longitude

Magnetometer – an instrument held manually or mounted on or suspended from an airplane to measure the strength and direction of the earth's magnetic field

Mercator, Gerardus (1512–1594) – a cartographer born in Antwerp (present-day Belgium) who created new designs for maps, developed the concept of the atlas, and devised a famous map projection very useful for navigators

Meteorologist – a person who studies and records the weather, often using and producing maps. Meteorologists also make weather forecasts

Nucleotide bases – Nucleotides are the chemical compounds that make up a *DNA* molecule. Each

nucleotide consists of three units: deoxyribose (a sugar molecule), a phosphate group, and one of four different nitrogen-containing compounds called bases

Panchromatic images – images taken using film or a sensor that records light, the visible part of the spectrum only

Pictogram – a chart or diagram in which symbols represent values. On a chart showing the birthrate in an area, a simple drawing of a baby might represent 10,000 births, three babies 30,000 births, and so on.

Pixel – short for "picture element"; the small "building block" of a *raster* image. Raster images consist entirely of regularly shaped small pixels, which, when viewed together, give the impression of a continuous image. Each pixel presents one shade or color in the image

Planetarium – a dome-shaped building in which projectors produce a representation of the night sky on the inside for an audience to view

Plate tectonics – the study of the movements of the plates or sections that make up the earth's crust. These plates ride on the semimolten rock inside the crust

Ptolemy – a Greek mathematician and geographer who lived in Alexandria, Egypt from about 90 to 168 A.D.; he was among the first scientists to study and develop map projections, and he also

wrote textbooks about how to make maps and how to collect information for them. The rediscovery of his works by European scholars in the 15th century stimulated the study of cartography

Raster data – image data made up of *pixels* plus associated information

Reflectance – a measure of the ability of a surface to reflect light or other radiation

Registration – the task of ensuring that map data sets correspond with each other and can be overlaid; checking that the data layers have the same *coordinate* system and projection. Similarly, when an image is printed, the *pixels* on the separate pieces of color film can be "out of register" if the films are not placed exactly on top of each other

Remote sensing – the taking of digital pictures of the earth from orbiting satellites

Resolution – the size of the *pixels* in a *raster* image relative to the true size of the object recorded. A satellite image showing pixels equivalent to 1000 meters on the earth is a low-resolution image compared to an image with a 10-meter pixel resolution

Scanning – sweeping across an image or part of the earth's surface with a device that can sense and record variation in the light

Software – computer programs that run the operation of computer hardware (parts of the computer)

Spectral signatures – the characteristic shape of the curve on a graph showing *reflectance* of an object of different parts of the *spectrum*

Spectrum – the electro-magnetic spectrum comprises the radiation of the colors of light visible to the human eye along with all other invisible waves emitted, such as x-rays and ultraviolet light

Thematic map – a map that shows one particular aspect of the natural or human environment such as transportation routes, weather patterns, tourism, population, vegetation, or geology

Topographic map – a map that shows natural features such as hills, rivers, and forests, and man-made features such as roads and buildings

Utilities – companies responsible for delivering services such as electricity, telephone, water, and gas supplies

Vector data – digital data made up of a set of *coordinates* plus associated information. Mapping vector data is a digital record of points, lines, and areas held in a *database*

Virtual environment – artificially created computerized data that, with the correct software, creates the impression of the real world; the best example is the virtual training cockpit of an airplane used in flight simulation

Warping – a form of *registration*; distorting an image to make it fit the *coordinate* system of another data set

Further Reading and Websites

Barber, Peter, ed. *The Lie of the Land*, British Library Publishing, 2001

Driver, Cline *Early American Maps and Views*, University Press of Virginia, 1988

Forte, I., et al., *Map Skills and Geography: Inventive Exercises to Sharpen Skills and Raise Achievement*, Incentive Publications, 1998

Haywood, John, et al., *Atlas of World History*, Barnes & Noble Books, 2001

Letham, Lawrence *GPS Made Easy*, Rocky Mountain Books, 1998

Monmonier, Mark *How to Lie with Maps*, University of Chicago Press, 1991

Monmonier, Mark *Map Appreciation*, Prentice Hall, 1988

Meltzer, M. *Columbus and the World around Him*, Franklin Watts, 1990

Stefoff, Rebecca *Young Oxford Companion to Maps and Mapmaking*, Oxford University Press, 1995

Thrower, Norman J. W. *Maps and Civilization: Cartography in Culture and Society*, 2nd ed., University of Chicago Press, 1999

Wilford, John. N. *The Mapmakers*, Pimlico, 2002

www.auslig.gov.au/
National mapping division of Australia. Find an aerial photograph of any area of the country

http://cgdi.gc.ca/ccatlas/atlas.htm
Internet-based Canadian Communities Atlas project. Schools create their own atlas

www.earthamaps.com/
Search by place name for U.S. city maps, with zoom facility

http://earthtrends.wri.org
World Resources Institute mapping of energy resources, agriculture, forestry, government, climate, and other thematic maps

http://geography.about.com
Links to pages on cartography, historic maps, GIS, and GPS; print out blank and outline maps for study purposes

http://ihr.sas.ac.uk/maps/
History of cartography; no images, but search for links to many other cartographic topics

www.lib.utexas.edu/maps/
Vast map collection at the University of Texas, historical and modern, including maps produced by the CIA

www.lib.virginia.edu/exhibits/lewis_clark/
Information on historic expeditions, including Lewis and Clark

www.lindahall.org/pubserv/hos/stars/
Exhibition of the Golden Age of the celestial atlas, 1482–1851

www.LivGenMI.com/1895.htm
A U.S. atlas first printed in 1895. Search for your town, city, or county

http://memory.loc.gov/ammem/gmdhtml/
Map collections 1500–1999, the Library of Congress; U.S. maps, including military campaigns and exploration

www.nationalgeographic.com/education/maps_geography/
The National Geographic educational site

http://oddens.geog.uu.nl/index.html
15,500 cartographic links; search by country or keyword

www.ordsvy.gov.uk/
Site of one of the oldest national mapping agencies. Search for and download historical and modern mapping of the U.K. Go to Understand Mapping page for cartographic glossary

www.mapzone.co.uk/
Competitions and quizzes for younger readers about Great Britain; site run by Ordnance Survey

http://www.libs.uga.edu/darchive/hargrett/maps/maps.html
University of Georgia historical map collection; maps from the 16th to the early 20th century

http://topozone.com/
Search by place name or latitude and longitude for all areas of the U.S. Maps at various scales

www.un.org/Depts/Cartographic/english/htmain.htm
United Nations cartographic section. Search by country and by different UN missions worldwide

http://mapping.usgs.gov/
U.S. national atlas and much more, including satellite images

http://interactive2.usgs.gov/learningweb/students/homework_geography.asp
USGS site for students; all kinds of useful information. Create your own map by plotting latitude and longitude coordinates

www.worldatlas.com/
World atlas and lots of statistics about all countries of the world

Set Index

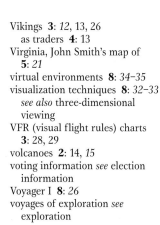

Picture Credits

Abbreviation: SPL   Science Photo Library

Jacket images Oblique view of antique map (background), Ken Reid/Telegraph Colour Library/Getty Images; T-in-O map of the world drawn in 1450 (inset, top), AKG London; three-dimensional map of the topography of Mars (inset, bottom), NASA/SPL; **9** Shane Murnion using Arc-Info mapping software (boris.qub.ac. uk/shane/arc/); **10, 11** City of La Grande, Oregon; **13** Roger Ressmeyer/Corbis; **14** Patrick Bennett/Corbis; **15** Joel W. Rogers/Corbis; **17** Alfred Pasieka/SPL; **19** Space Imaging Europe/SPL; **22** Earth Satellite Corporation/SPL; **23t, 23b, 24, 25t** NASA/SPL; **25b** Frank Zullo/SPL; **26** Peter Ryan/SPL; **26-27, 28l** NASA/SPL; **28r** Earth Satellite Corporation/SPL; **29t** BP/NRSC/SPL; **29b** Margaret S. Watters; **30** Alfred Pasieka/SPL; **31l** P.A. McTurk, University of Leicester & David Parker/SPL; **31r** Peter Menzel/SPL; **33** 2000 OSU Spatial Climate Analysis Service/The Climate Source; **34** David Parker/SPL; **35l** James King-Holmes/SPL; **35r** Geoff Tompkinson/SPL; **36** U.S. Geological Survey; **37t** AFP Photo; **37b** Sittler, Jerrican/SPL.

While every effort has been made to trace the copyright holders of illustrations reproduced in this book, the publishers will be pleased to rectify any omissions or inaccuracies.